They Aren't Broken, They Are Beautiful

Living with Autism

Table of Contents

Introduction

Chapter 1: What Is Autistic Spectrum Disorder?

Catching the Signs in a Baby or Toddler

Catching the Signs in an Older Child

Inflexible Signs

Chapter 2: Different Types of Autism

Asperger's Syndrome

Rett Syndrome

CDD - Childhood Disintegrative Disorder

Kanner's Syndrome

PDD-NOS - Pervasive Developmental Disorder - Not Otherwise Specified

Chapter 3: Living with Autism

References

They Aren't Broken, They Are Beautiful

Introduction

So, your child has been diagnosed as having Autistic Spectrum Disorder. You know it, but you've probably lost count of how many times people have said to you, 'your child doesn't look autistic.' How is an autistic child meant to look? Should they have a sign on their heads saying, 'I am autistic?' The answer to that is a resounding no, but it's scary how many people don't know what autism is and how many think that anyone with a 'disorder' of any kind should look physically different.

They Aren't Broken, They Are Beautiful

Chapter 1: What Is Autistic Spectrum Disorder?

Many parents panic when their child is diagnosed, but that's mainly because they don't really understand what it is. It is called a spectrum disorder because there is a spectrum of symptoms. ASD generally makes itself known in the early years, and it gets picked up on because of a lack of development, such as a delay in talking and playing.

The signs of autism vary, and not every child will share the same ones. However, it is generally acknowledged that the three primary areas affected are:

- Verbal and non-verbal communication

- Interacting and relating with others around them

- Flexible thought and behavior

While the signs vary, what doesn't is the opinion that the earlier they are caught, the easier it is to treat. Spotting the Warning Signs

As a parent, you are in best-placed to spot the early signs. Nobody knows your child the way you do, and nobody spends as much time with them as you.

- **Monitoring Development** - Autism revolves around

developmental delays, so monitoring your child to see if they hit the cognitive, social, and emotional milestones is important. Although every child develops at a different pace and delays may not automatically mean ASD, there is a good chance it is.

• **Concerned? Speak to Someone** - If your child seems to be lagging in talking and walking, don't panic. However, if you are concerned that your child is not developing as they should, speak to your health care provider and pediatrician immediately. If they tell you to wait and see, don't. Autistic children don't grow out of their symptoms and will likely need additional help.

• **Trust Your Own Instincts** - Hopefully, your doctor will listen to you and will thoroughly examine your child. However, they don't always spot the signs, so if your gut tells you something is wrong, follow it up. Be persistent - it's your child, and you want the best for them. If necessary, ask to be referred to a specialist in child development.

A major red flag is regression. If your child has developed normally, talking, and playing as normal, and then suddenly stops, or if you notice any apparent regression in social skills, you need to take it seriously and seek help immediately.

Catching the Signs in a Baby or Toddler

When autism is caught at an early enough age, your child's mind is flexible enough to benefit from the treatment. Although diagnosis before 2 years of age is tough, there are some signs you can pick up on before then. Some of those signs are:

- Not making eye contact or smiling

- Not responding to your voice or their name

- Not visually following objects or gestures

- Not using gestures to communicate

- Not making any noise to attract your attention

- Not responding to cuddling

- Not imitating your facial expressions or movements

- Not playing with others

Catching the Signs in an Older Child

The older a child gets, the more diverse the signs and they usually revolve around social difficulties:

They Aren't Broken, They Are Beautiful

- Lack of interest or awareness of anyone or anything around them

- Unaware of how to make friends, play or connect with other people

- Doesn't like being cuddled or touched

- Doesn't get involved in group games, use toys creatively or play 'make-believe' games

- Struggles to understand and talk about feelings

- Doesn't appear to hear others

- Doesn't share achievements or interests with others

Signs of language (verbal and non-verbal) and speech difficulties may also become apparent, including:

- Speaks in an odd rhythm or an atypical tone

- Repeats phrases and words with no real intent

- Repeats a question instead of answering it

- Doesn't use language correctly or refers to themselves in the third person

• Doesn't understand sarcasm or irony and takes every spoken word literally

• Doesn't make eye contact

• Facial expressions don't match their words

• Doesn't appear aware of people's gestures, voice tone, or facial expressions

• Doesn't make many gestures and appears almost robot-like

• May show sensitivity to sounds, textures, smells, and sights

Inflexible Signs

Other signs include:

• Following a rigid routine, such as sticking to one route only to go to school

• Struggle to adapt to environmental or schedule changes

• Forms unusual attachments to certain objects, arranges things in a certain order, or lines up objects

• Preoccupied with a small topic, usually anything involving symbols or numbers

• Repeats movements or actions over and again, such as rocking, shaking hands, etc.

Of course, there are many more signs and symptoms, and only you, as their parent, can know if something appears to be wrong with your child's development.

Chapter 2: Different Types of Autism

Autism isn't a one-size-fits-all disorder. To ensure your child gets the right help and care, you need to understand the different types of autism and their respective signs. Only when you know what type of autism your child has can you ensure they get everything they - and you - need. There are five primary types:

Asperger's Syndrome

Perhaps one of the better-known types of autism, the term Asperger's Syndrome, is no longer used by medical professionals. Now, they call it Level-1 Autism Spectrum Disorder, although many people still call it Asperger's.

A child with Asperger's will be strong in their verbal skills and have more than average intelligence. However, they will struggle with social communication and, generally, you can expect to see the following symptoms:

- Inflexible behavior and thought

- Struggle to move from one activity to another

- Struggle with executive functioning

- Speech is flat and monotone, and they struggle to change pitch or use speech to express their feelings

- Struggle to interact with peers at home or school

Rett Syndrome

Typically noticed in infants, Rett's is a rare neurological disorder that affects girls more than boys. The challenges brought about by Rett's can affect every aspect of your child's life. However, that won't affect their enjoyment of life, and they can live a full and happy life with the right care. Common signs include:

- Loss of normal movement and coordination

- Speech and communication struggles

- In some cases, breathing problems

CDD - Childhood Disintegrative Disorder

CDD is also called disintegrative psychosis and Heller's Syndrome. It is a neurodevelopmental disorder typically signified by problems in certain developmental areas, including social function, motor skills, and language. Mostly, this disorder does not become known until the child is between 3 and 10 years old - up to that point, their development is normal. This is one of the hardest disorders for parents to cope with - seeing their child lose all their hard-fought-for development is heartbreaking, especially as they had no idea their child was struggling with autism all along. What causes CDD is largely unknown but has been linked to the brain's neurobiology. It is also not really known why it affects boys more than girls - out of every 10 cases, 9 will be boys. When a child begins to regress, it will typically be in at least two developmental aspects, and they may lose any or all of these learned abilities and skills:

- Vocabulary and language

- Toilet skills (were already learned)

- Adaptive behaviors and social skills

- Some of their motor skills

Kanner's Syndrome

Leo Kanner discovered this syndrome in 1943 when he worked as a psychiatrist at John Hopkins University. He originally characterized Kanner's Syndrome as infantile autism, and it is described today as classic autism. Children who have Kanner's appear to be alert, intelligent, and attractive but will have some or all of the following characteristics:

- They won't form emotional attachments with anyone

• They struggle with interaction and communication

• Their speech is uncontrolled

• They are obsessed with handling certain objects

• They have visuospatial skills and rote memory and find it hard to learn in some areas

PDD-NOS - Pervasive Developmental Disorder - Not Otherwise Specified

PDD is one of the milder autism types with a range of different symptoms, commonly in language and social development. Your child may struggle to develop their language and motor skills and may be delayed in learning to walk. You can also identify it by watching your child and making a note of the areas they struggle in, such as interaction with peers. This type of autism is sometimes known as subthreshold autism, referring to an individual who only has some autistic traits.

They Aren't Broken, They Are Beautiful

Chapter 3: Living with Autism

As a parent, you've probably already given a great deal of thought to your child's future already, and if they are diagnosed with ASD, you've spent a lot more time thinking about the future than a parent without an autistic child likely would.

It isn't just the worry about your child's medical care and any therapies they may need; you will also worry about how you will cope in the months and years ahead. Your whole life will change for a while, and it may seem tough.

But it shouldn't be. Sure, things will have to change, but there are many things you can do every day to make life easier for you, your child, and the rest of your family.

Stay Focused on the Positive - All children respond to positive reinforcement, especially autistic children. Praise them when they do something well; not only will it make your child feel better, but their reaction will warm you from the inside out.

Be Specific -Tell them exactly what they did well and why. And don't forget to reward them - extra time for playing, an extra bedtime story, etc. Even small prizes like stickers work well.

Love Your Child for Who They Are - All children love to be prized for who they are, and this is especially key for children on the spectrum.

They Aren't Broken, They Are Beautiful

Be Consistent and Keep to a Schedule - Autistic children need schedules and struggle to function if they deviate from them. Also, be consistent with your child in interaction, guidance, and in your schedule to help them learn to cope. It also ensures they find it easier to learn new behaviors and skills and learn how to apply what they learn when they face different situations. Get together with your child's therapists and teachers to ensure you are all aligned and consistent on a set of interaction methods and techniques - that way, what they learn at school can be continued at home, and vice versa.

Include Playtime on Their Schedule - Growing up isn't just about learning through lessons; it's also about learning through playtime. Find activities that your child finds fun, activities not based on learning and education, to give your child a break, to help you bond, and help you both connect better.

Give It Time - The first things you try may not work. There are many treatments, therapies, techniques, and approaches, and you are likely to try a lot of them before you find what works for both of you. Always stay positive, even when something doesn't seem to work, and don't get discouraged. If something isn't working, try something else.

Include Your Child in Daily Activities - This is important, especially if your child exhibits unpredictable behavior. Sometimes, it's easier to take them with you than leave them exposed to situations where they may not be able to cope, and including them in your grocery shops or trips to town will help them get used to the outside world and being surrounded by strangers.

They Aren't Broken, They Are Beautiful

Make Sure You Have Support - It doesn't matter whether it is online help, friends, health professionals, or other families with an autistic child. Make sure you surround yourself with plenty of support from others who understand what having an autistic child is like and how hard it can be at times. You can use this group to get help, advice, useful information, and share good and bad times. You may need to consider marital counseling if you and your spouse are struggling, family counseling, and even individual counseling. Do whatever it takes to make life a little easier for you, and never be afraid to ask for help when you need it.

Think About Respite Care - There will be times when you need a break. Looking after an autistic child can be mentally, physically, and emotionally draining. You may need to consider having a caregiver take over for a while - in the home and outside. This will be ore the case where your child has intense requirements, and it can give you the time you need to take a breather, recharge your batteries, and do something you really enjoy. That way, when you return home, you are better equipped to continue helping your child. There are lots of ways to form a respite team:

- o See if friends and family familiar with your child can help or can give you advice about support ideas you may not have considered.

- o Speak to your child's doctor, teachers, and therapists to see if they have any ideas or caregivers, they can refer you to. If your child gets on particularly well with a specific teacher's aide and you like them too, they may be able to give you a break, even if it's just for a few hours.

- o Find online support groups and post notices for help, or post them in newspapers or local universities and colleges. Make sure you get references and check them all out thoroughly before you allow a stranger to take care of your child.

- o Join a support group and talk to others about what they do.

- o If you do decide to take on a caregiver, make sure you spend time introducing them to your child and vice versa if they are strangers. That way, it won't be such a shock when you disappear for a while and someone else takes over.

Look After Yourself - Parenting is hard enough at the best of times, but it can be even harder when you have an autistic child. You need to keep yourself healthy - physically and mentally - to ensure you are capable of facing the daily challenges. This means you need to find ways of taking care of yourself and letting others help - you don't need to do it all alone. And don't forget the rest of your family - they need you too.

Reduce Your Stress - Having an autistic child can bring on a lot of stress, far more than some parents experience looking after children with other disabilities. Unchecked stress can lead to family breakdowns and affect your physical health and mental health. Ensuring you are organized can help, which means you need to make time for yourself. These tips can help you do this:

- o Work out what is causing the stress. Break the bigger issues into smaller ones and make a plan on how to deal with them

- o Try meditation. Focus on your thoughts and think about how you talk to yourself. You will be able to work out what worries are not real and discard them.

They Aren't Broken, They Are Beautiful

- o Get some exercise in. You don't have to join an exercise class or gym unless you want to; going for a walk can help just as well, especially if you have a dog or can borrow one from a friend.

- o Get plenty of sleep. Sleep helps your body recharge and makes it easier to face the day ahead. If you struggle to drop off to sleep or night or don't sleep well, try meditation, take a warm bath, or do some relaxation exercises just before bed.

- o Be creative with meals. A healthy diet is as important as a good night's sleep. You are likely already taking the time to ensure your child eats a nutritious diet, so make sure you do the same. Mix things up a little and get creative with your meals, adding in different fruits and vegetables to spice things up. And, very important when you have an autistic child, set a meal schedule, and stick to it.

Have Balance In Your Life - This will help you face challenges that come your way and ensure you have a good quality of life. Make time to socialize and have fun:

- o Get together with friends, even if it's just for a coffee, and catch up once a week.

- o Take up a hobby. If you used to knit or sew, start again. Learn to play an instrument or join the local golf club.

- o Take time for yourself every day. Taking ten minutes for yourself in the morning can help you center yourself and be ready to face the day.

- o If your spouse, another family member, or friend can take over for a short while, take yourself off for a walk or head to the grocery store by yourself.

They Aren't Broken, They Beautiful

At the end of the day, no matter how you feel or what people say, remember this - **your child is not broken**. They are beautiful, inside, and out, and while you may be drained of energy, tired beyond belief, that is what will keep you going.

References

Fulghum, Debra. 2016. 'Tips for Parenting a Child on the Autism Spectrum.' WebMD. WebMD. December 23, 2016. https://www.webmd.com/brain/autism/parenting-child-with-autism.

Melinda. 2019. 'Does My Child Have Autism?' HelpGuide.org. March 20, 2019. https://www.helpguide.org/articles/autism-learning-disabilities/does-my-child-have-autism.htm.

'My Experience of Living with Autism.' 2019. Www.medicalnewstoday.com. May 24, 2019. https://www.medicalnewstoday.com/articles/325239.

'What Are the 5 Types of Autism?' n.d. https://www.integrityinc.org/what-are-the-5-types-of-autism

They Aren't Broken, They Are Beautiful

Write It Down, Leave It On The Page, BREATH

_____

_____

_____

_____

_____

_____

They Aren't Broken, They Are Beautiful

They Aren't Broken, They Are Beautiful

Made in the USA
Monee, IL
30 May 2022